Some are wild,
Some are tame.
Just turn the page
To learn their name.

This is my book.

My name is:

_____

_____

For all children everywhere,
but especially for Joy.

Noah liked a tidy ark.
Here's the way they disembark: (see previous page)

Aardvark Bear Camel Dog Elephant Fox Goose
Horse Impala Jaguar Kangaroo Lion Mouse Nilgai Owl Pig Quail
Rabbit Swan Tiger Unicorn Vicuna Whale Xiphosura Yak Zebra

The Christian ABC Book

Rhymes by John Foster

Art by June Goldsborough

Christianica Center • 1807 Prairie Street • Glenview, IL 60025

ISBM 0-911346-05-8   098765432

A is for Adam, the husband of Eve.
They were naughty in Eden so they had to leave.

The Bible has the full story
in Genesis 2:4-3:24

B is for Babel, the tower that stood
where men tried to reach heaven without being good.

Genesis 11:1-9

C is for Cain who was bad to his brother
and then ran away from his father and mother.

Genesis 4:1-16

D is for Daniel who wasn't afraid

for he knew that God's angel would come to his aid.

Daniel 6:1-29

E

is for Egypt where Moses was born
and was found in the bulrushes one early morn.

Exodus 1:1-2:10

F is for Family—sisters and brothers,
and Mommy and Daddy and maybe some others.

G is for Giant—Goliath was one.

He was wrong when he thought little David would run.

1 Samuel 17:1-58

H is for Helping—that's what we should do
for it makes people happy, and God happy, too.

Matthew 25:31-46

I is for Israel, home of the Jews

who were chosen by God to announce the Good News.

J is for Jesus who loves girls and boys
for he shares in our tears and he shares in our joys.

K is for Kindness—like giving a hug
to a playmate who's hurt when he trips on a rug.

L is for Lambs and for Laughter and Love.
They are presents to us from our Father above.

M is for Mothers, they hug us and squeeze us, and also for Mary, the mother of Jesus.

Luke 2:7

N is for Noah who gathered up two

of each creature on earth for his big floating zoo.

Genesis
6:5-8:22

O is for Old People—older than twenty.
Be patient with them for their problems are plenty.

P is for Prayers which we say every night,
and then Mommy will kiss us and tuck us in tight.

Q is for Queen—lovely Sheba was one.
She brought Solomon gifts that weighed more than a ton.

1 Kings 10:1-13

R is for Rainbow God puts in the sky
as a sign that the worst of the storm has gone by.

Genesis 9:8-17

S is for Shadrach, thrown into the fire.

God kept him so cool that he didn't perspire.

Daniel, Chapter 3

T is for Teacher who helps us to learn.

Every day when we leave her we want to return.

U is for Ugly which nobody is
because God made us all to be children of His.

V is for Valentine—that's what we send
when we want to be nice to a new little friend.

W stands for the little word, "We,"

and it's one of the best words—it means you and me.

X is for Xerxes, a bad king who changed

and then did all the good things Queen Esther arranged.

Esther 2:1-10:10

Y is for Yes, it's the word we should say
when we're asked to do something for others today.